D0728649

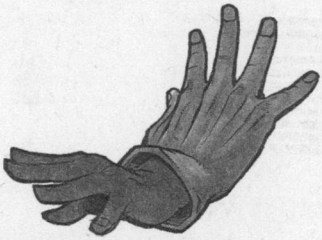

Volume 20! Thanks for picking it up! My little sister's friend's son is a fan of Jiro, and I hear he was influenced enough to start taking guitar lessons! Jiro is one rocking girl who can play both guitar and bass! Rock on, Kyoka Jiro!!

KOHEI HORIKOSHI

DISCARD

MY HERO ACADEMIA

20

SHONEN JUMP Manga Edition

STORY & ART **KOHEI HORIKOSHI**

TRANSLATION & ENGLISH ADAPTATION **Caleb Cook**
TOUCH-UP ART & LETTERING **John Hunt**
DESIGNER **Julian [JR] Robinson**
SHONEN JUMP SERIES EDITOR **John Bae**
GRAPHIC NOVEL EDITOR **Mike Montesa**

BOKU NO HERO ACADEMIA © 2014 by Kohei Horikoshi
All rights reserved.
First published in Japan in 2014 by SHUEISHA Inc., Tokyo.
English translation rights arranged by SHUEISHA Inc.

The stories, characters and incidents mentioned in this publication are entirely fictional.

No portion of this book may be reproduced or transmitted in any form
or by any means without written permission from the copyright holders.

Printed in the U.S.A.

Published by VIZ Media, LLC
P.O. Box 77010
San Francisco, CA 94107

10 9 8 7 6 5 4 3 2 1
First printing, August 2019

MY HERO ACADEMIA vol. 20

KOHEI HORIKOSHI

HEAD-HAIR SHUFFLE CHARACTER LINEUP!!

It's terrible!! Last time, the Meddler jumbled up class 1-A's brains and bodies. But this other guy named Swop T. Hairington lives across from the Meddler's parents' house, and he's causing trouble this time!!

His Quirk lets him shuffle people's hair around!! They're all having plenty of fun with their new dos!! Can you tell who's got whose style?!

One day, people began manifesting special abilities that came to be known as "Quirks," and before long, the world was full of superpowered humans. But with the advent of these exceptional individuals came an increase in crime, and governments alone were unable to deal with the situation. At the same time, others emerged to oppose the spread of evil! As if straight from the comic books, these heroes keep the peace and are even officially authorized to fight crime. Our story begins when a certain Quirkless boy and lifelong hero fan meets the world's number one hero, starting him on his path to becoming the greatest hero ever!

STORY

ANSWERS: (1) MINETA, (2) SHOJI, (3) IDA, (4) AIZAWA, (5) OJIRO, (6) SATO, (7) ALL MIGHT, (8) TODOROKI, (9) KIRISHIMA, (10) KAMINARI, (11) JIRO, (12) BAKUGO, (13) URARAKA, (14) ASHIDO, (15) YAOYOROZU, (16) TOKOYAMI, (17) ASUI, (18) AOYAMA, (19) SERO, (20) MIDORIYA, (21) HAGAKURE, (22) KODA

No.178 The Woman Called La Brava 7

No.179 School Festival Start!! 25

No.180 Unbeknownst 43

No.181 For Someone Else 61

No.182 Let It Flow! School Festival! 77

No.183 Festival All Day Long!! 97

No.184 Japanese Hero Billboard Chart 115

No.185 Wing Hero: Hawks 133

No.186 Endeavor and Hawks 148

No.187 Flaming Roar! vs. Nomu: High-End 169

No.188 Your Father, the Number One Hero 187

SEXY.
NOT WHAT I'D EXPECT FROM SUCH A VIOLENT GAL!
HA HA HA HA HA HA HA HA
Ooh!!
BWA HA HA HA! WHAT'S WITH THAT GETUP, KENDO?!
No. 178 - The Woman Called La Brava
A COMPLIMENT, OF COURSE!! I'M THE ONE WHO ENTERED YOU INTO THIS THING IN THE FIRST PLACE!!
RUSH RUSH
AND YOU BOYS HAD BETTER STOP RUSHING IN HERE.
1-B PREP ROOM
IS THAT A COMPLIMENT OR AN INSULT?
AND ONCE YOU DO, THAT'LL MAKE CLASS 1-B EVEN MORE PLUS ULTRA!
YOU'RE SURE TO WIN, SINCE THAT COMMERCIAL MADE YOU SO POPULAR!
HEY, HEY, HANG ON NOW. ARE YOU SURE SHE'LL WIN?
WHY ARE YOU SO CONFI-DENT?
NEJIRE HADO!
BEEP
BUT MORE IMPORTANTLY, I GET A REPRIEVE FROM YOUR WICKED SWINGS IN THE MEANTIME!!
HA HA HA HA HA HA
WELL... IF I'M GONNA DO IT, MIGHT AS WELL TRY TO WIN.

FWIP FWIP
Not if you're talking about winners!!
Oh my. Don't count me out just yet!

I'M HAPPY TO BE COMPETING WITH YOU, KENDO!

BIBIMI KENRANZAKI !!
For I am the ultimate beauty here...
OHOHO OHOHO

BATTLE OF THE BABES!
Oho ho ho ho ho ho ho!

...AND CLASS B'S SHOW COMES RIGHT AFTER THAT.
CLASS A'S PERFORMANCE STARTS AT TEN...
THEN LUNCH, THEN THE BEAUTY PAGEANT.
Perfect Guide

TAXI
ALMOST THERE.

YEAH ...!
WE SURE ARE EXCITED TO SEE MIDORIYA, RIGHT, ERI?
MORN-ING.
GOOD MORNING! WHAT ARE YOU UP TO?
WHAT? I'M IN PEAK CONDITION RIGHT NOW!!
HATSUME. YOU, UM, MIGHT WANT TO FIX YOURSELF UP BEFORE THE PRESENTATION.
HE HEADED DOWN THE HILL TO GO SHOPPING.
YEAH. THE BOY HAD TWO OR THREE THINGS HE HAD TO PICK UP.
PLUCK
TODAY ?!
PERMISSION TO LEAVE THE GROUNDS?
Better not turn my head.
YOUTHFUL ENTHUSIASM I GET, BUT COME ON...
WITH EVERYTHING ABOUT TO START? HE'S KINDA CUTTING IT CLOSE...

No. 178 - The Woman Called La Brava

BOING
...UNTIL OUR GRAND EXIT, YET...
I HAD HOPED TO SAVE YOUR QUIRK...
BUT, BUT!! AT THIS RATE OUR WHOLE PLAN WILL BE RUINED!
BOING
SKF
...I HAVE NO CHOICE BUT TO ASK THIS OF YOU, LA BRAVA.
AS WE'RE UNDER A TIME LIMIT ...
I AM WELL AWARE!!
AMP
ALREADY HERE?!
WATCH CLOSELY!

DODGING MY AIR BLAST THREW OFF HIS FORM.
BOING!
BWOOM
...HE THREW UP ANOTHER AIR BARRIER IN ORDER TO LAND.
WHILE RIGHTING HIMSELF ...
I NOTED THE EXACT SPOT...
WORMP
ON TOP OF THIS TREE!!

BOING
BWOOF
...AND REMEMBERED.
SWIP
NNGH!

HAHH !!
FWOOM
OOMF
SHP
?!
THROB
!!
GAH!

SLAM

I CANNOT MOVE A MUSCLE ...!!
GUGH

JUST GIVE UP, BOTH OF YOU!
YOU'D BETTER NOT RESIST EITHER, MISS!

I STAKE MY VERY BEARD AND SOUL ON THIS CAPER.
NORMALLY, GENTLE KNOWS IT'S TIME TO TURN TAIL WHEN WE GET SPOTTED ...!!

NOW THAT DETERMINATION'S BACKFIRING...!!
OH, GENTLE ...!!
FOR REAL?!
I HAVEN'T EVEN SPOKEN TWO WORDS TO HER, BUT SHE SENT ME A LOVE LETTER.
YOU KNOW AIBA, IN CLASS 3? THE TINY ONE?
YEARBOOK
FIRST SUMMER BREAK IN MIDDLE SCHOOL...
SCARY! SOUNDS LIKE A STALKER TO ME!!
THAT GIRL WROTE OUT DOZENS OF PAGES OF THAT CRAP...
SHE WENT ON ABOUT HOW COOL I AM WHEN I DO THIS AND THAT...
GET THIS ...
PRETTY OBVIOUS SHE'S BEEN FOLLOWING ME AROUND.

AFTER THAT, I DIDN'T LET MYSELF BELIEVE IN ANYONE OR ANYTHING.
I FOUND THE COURAGE TO CONFESS TO THE BOY I LIKED AND GOT MOCKED FOR IT.

GREET-INGS, VIEWERS ...
BUT THEN I FOUND HIM...

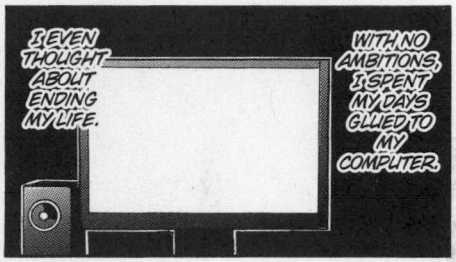
I EVEN THOUGHT ABOUT ENDING MY LIFE.
WITH NO AMBITIONS, I SPENT MY DAYS GLUED TO MY COMPUTER.

I FOUND YOU.
MY LIGHT.
YES, IT IS I! GENTLE!! GENTLE CRIMINAL!!
DISSATISFIED WITH THE STATE OF THINGS? I SHALL GIVE YOU SOMETHING TO BELIEVE IN!!
YES!! I PLAN TO CHANGE THIS WORLD OF OURS!!

I SURE HOPE HE DOESN'T THINK THEY'RE GROSS.
THERE'S NOTHING I CAN DO ABOUT THESE DARK RINGS.

GENTLE CRIMINAL.

BUT YOU NEVER SAID A WORD. YOU ACCEPTED ME FOR ME.

CODE NAME LA BRAVA. WHAT DO YOU SAY?
MISS MANAMI AIBA.

Hot compress

GENTLE!! MY DEAR GENTLE!

IN MY ESTIMATION, WE MAKE THE PERFECT TEAM.

I'M HANDING YOU OVER TO THE POLICE.
THEY'LL BE HERE SOON.
LA BRAVA
I LOVE YOU.
QUIRK:
THANK YOU.
LA BRAVA.
LOVE

UPON UTTERING THE WORD LOVE...
GUH
KUH
WHERE'S ...
...THIS POWER COMING FROM?
...THE PERSON SHE LOVES MOST...
KUH
KUH
KUH
...RECEIVES A TEMPORARY POWER BOOST!
THE DEEPER THE LOVE, THE STRONGER THE BOOST.
APOLOGIES, BOY.
AND WHEN IT ACTIVATES IN MOMENTS OF CRISIS...
FWISH
I PREFER NOT TO RESOLVE MATTERS BY FORCE ...

WHICH IS WHY...
...I ALWAYS EDIT OUT THIS PART.
...THE TARGET GROWS DOZENS OF TIMES STRONGER.
ENJOY A NICE NAP, IF YOU WILL.

SORRY ABOUT THIS, IZUKU MIDORIYA.

BUT IN THE END, LOVE ALWAYS TRIUMPHS.
DAM
...STRONGER... AND FASTER THAN YOU...
I'VE FOUGHT... PLENTY OF PEOPLE...
AND I HAVEN'T LOST YET!

THE CONTRIBUTION

We made it to volume 20! I've been drawing this for four years straight! And it's all thanks to you—the readers!! In this book, we've even got congratulatory art from two other artists!!

The first one, you're probably already familiar with—Betten Court is the artist for the spin-off series in *Jump+*, *My Hero Academia: Vigilantes*!! When they first told me, "You're getting a full-blown spin-off drawn by Betten Court," I was dumbstruck. It was especially awe-inspiring and a little scary to hear, since as a kid, I regularly read *Prince Standard* and *Ashita Dorobo*. Thank you so much for getting involved with *MHA*, Betten Sensei!

The other is Yoko Akiyama, who has her own serialization in *Jump+* called *Saguri-chan Tankentai*!! She started out as an assistant helping me with *MHA*, and from the outset, it was almost frustrating just how good she was at drawing cute girls. I'd grind my teeth and stew over the quality of her drawings, seriously. Thank you for all you've done and continue to do, Akiyama Sensei!!

Volume 5 of *Vigilantes* and volume 3 of *Saguri-chan* released at the same time as this book in Japan. They both have some illustrations from me, so if you're interested, go ahead and check those out! Doing art swaps like this is so exciting! I love it!

Good Mooornin'!
No. 179 - School Festival Start!!
Hey, guys!! Hope you're ready, cuz it's finally time!!
Aw, yeah. Here we go.
*U.A. Amusement Park Signs: Class 2-D's Quirky Attraction
Sniff
Sniff
Sniff
Today's the day when class year and department don't matter— we're all just here to cut loose!!
Now say it with me, everyone.

LET THE U.A. ...
POP
9:00 A.M.
BWOOM
... BEEE ...

...
SCHOOL
FESTIVAL
...
POP
FESTIVAL
NO. 179 - SCHOOL FESTIVAL START!!
...
GIINN
!!

HOW'D HE...?!
UNTHINKABLE, BOY!!
FLIP
PLEASE!
USING OUR LOVER MODE TO OVERCOME THE ODDS!!
SWIP
A LAST RESORT, JUST LIKE ALWAYS...!!

STOP THIS, PLEASE !!
AS ALWAYS !!
THE TWO OF US!!
...WASN'T STRONG ENOUGH!!
MY LOVE...
GENTLE, I'M SO, SO, SORRY!!
...THAT YOUR FEELINGS FOR ME ARE INADEQUATE!
NOT A SINGLE SOUL HAS YET TO PROVE...

...SANDWICH!!
GENTLY...
URK!!
THUD!
SHK
...!!
SO I AM LOATH TO STACK THEM LIKE THIS.
THE THINNER THE SANDWICH, THE CLASSIER IT IS, INHERENTLY...
THE FLEETING DREAM OF A MAN PAST HIS YOUTH.
GUH
AND YET, I MUST SEE THIS THROUGH.

"WHO'RE YOU, AGAIN?"
"AH... UMM..."
AND THIS DREAM IS NO LONGER MINE ALONE.
...WILL GIVE A MOMENT'S THOUGHT TO THE WAY I LIVED AND BE INSPIRED.
SO THAT GOING FORWARD, SOMEONE OUT THERE...
TO CARVE MY NAME IN HISTORY, FOR FUTURE GENERATIONS!
MY DREAM WOULD BE TRIFLING INDEED IF YOUR WORDS COULD MOVE ME TO ABANDON MY COURSE!
TODAY MARKS MY FIRST STEP TOWARD TRUE INFAMY.
BOOM
...MY PENCHANT FOR DREAMING.
...I ASSUME YOU CAN COMPRE-HEND...
AS YOU ARE A U.A. STUDENT ...
SHP

THOOM
SO WHY?
AND THIS DREAM IS NO LONGER MINE ALONE.
SHP
FLIP
WHY TRAMPLE ALL OVER OUR FEELINGS? OUR HOPES AND DREAMS?!
IF YOU GET IT, THEN WHY ATTACK OUR FESTIVAL?!

WORMMP
GLUH
?!
TOMP
ZWF
FWOOF
SUCH IS THE WAY OF THE WORLD!!

ZOOM
GAH!
YOU'D STEAL A SMILE FROM A GIRL WHO DOESN'T KNOW THE MEANING OF JOY YET?!
FOR YOUR DREAM, HUH? SO YOU'D RUIN ALL OUR HARD WORK? OUR PASSION?!
...IS WHAT IT TAKES.
IF THAT...

ONE WITH ENOUGH GREAT DEEDS TO LAND ME IN THE TEXTBOOKS.
GENTLE, AT 18 (HIGH SCHOOL SECOND-YEAR)
I HOPE TO BECOME A HERO.
DREAMS ...
WHAT'S MORE, THIS MAKES FOUR TIMES YOU'VE FLUNKED THE PROVISIONAL LICENSE EXAM.
AT THIS POINT, I HAVE TO RECOMMEND THAT YOU DROP OUT ALTOGETHER.
YOU GOT HELD BACK A YEAR BECAUSE YOU FAILED, AND OURS ISN'T EVEN A HIGH-LEVEL SCHOOL.
YOU AREN'T LISTENING, SO I'LL TELL IT TO YOU STRAIGHT, TOBITA.
I HEAR TAKESHITA ALREADY GOT SOME OFFERS FROM AGENCIES.
FEAR NOT, MOTHER.
I WILL ENDURE, UNDAUNTED!!

MY QUIRK COULD HAVE CUSHIONED HIS FALL.
HE'S FALLING!!
UP THERE !!
OH NO!!
Caffe
HUHH ?!
BOING
SUCH WAS MY JUDGMENT CALL!
THAT'S ONE CHARGE OF OBSTRUCTING PUBLIC DUTIES...
AS IT HAPPENED, YOU PREVENTED THE HERO FROM EXECUTING THE RESCUE.
THE MAN WHO FELL WILL NEED SIX MONTHS TO MAKE A FULL RECOVERY.
*GRAFFITI: SCUM, TRASH
Expulsion Notice

I'D LONG SINCE FORGOTTEN MY DREAMS!
THE REASON FOR EATING TSUKUSHI.
SPRING. LOVELY.
HEH HEH...
SWAY
GENTLE, AT 22 (UNDEREMPLOYED)
SPRING
*TSUKUSHI IS A WILD MOUNTAIN VEGETABLE AVAILABLE IN SPRING.
YAP
YAP
I DIDN'T HAVE THE LUXURY OF PAYING THEM A PASSING THOUGHT...
YOU REMEMBER ME, OF COURSE?!
WE WERE IN THE SAME CLASS, THOUGH I WAS HELD BACK A YEAR!
YOU'VE GONE INDEPENDENT, THEN?! HOW FANTASTIC!!
TAKESHITA?! WHY, IF IT ISN'T TAKESHITA!!

WHO'RE YOU, AGAIN?
AH... UMM...
...TO LAND
...ARE DEAD.
ONE WITH
EN MY H
DREAMS...
DEEDS...
I SAY NAY!!
HISTORY OF SUPERVILLAINY
TO WITHER AND ROT ON THE VINE, LIKE THIS?!
IS IT MY MISERABLE FATE TO LIVE IN SQUALOR?

NOT JUST YET!!
SURE, HE REFLECTS PEOPLE'S ATTACKS BACK AT 'EM, BUT ALWAYS JUST TO MAKE A GETAWAY!!
WE'VE USED LOVER MODE MORE TIMES THAN I CAN COUNT!
GENTLE!
I CAN LIVE WITH THAT!!
YOU FIND ME UNPRINCIPLED? MOCK ME IF YOU MUST!!
MY GENTLE DOESN'T APPROVE OF VIOLENCE.

NOBODY'S MOCKING YOU, GENTLE CRIMINAL.

YOU CAN WIN THIS!!
GENTLE!!
FWOOSH

Congratulations on the MHA movie and volume 20!!
Better
20

YOU CAN WIN THIS...
...GENTLE!
No. 180 - UNBEKNOWNST

THE STEAM FROM HER QUIRK...
SHP

NOBODY'S MOCKING YOU... GENTLE CRIMINAL!

HE'S GETTING STRON-GER!
MORE KEEPS COMING OUT!

I REMEMBER NOW, GENTLE!! THAT KID'S IZUKU MIDORIYA. HE FOUGHT AT THE SPORTS FESTIVAL...
HE'S MAD, THEN!
NOT ONE TO ENTANGLE OURSELVES WITH!!
BOY!!
WHY DO YOU ...
GUH
...HOPE TO BECOME A HERO ?!
...
KR
THROB
AK

THIS DREAM IS NO LONGER MINE ALONE.
I LOVE YOU.
WE'RE NOT SO DIFFERENT, GENTLE!
BOP
THERE ARE PEOPLE WHO RESPECTED ME FOR IT! I GOTTA HONOR THAT!
IT WAS ONE I'D TOTALLY GIVEN UP ON! BUT I HAD PEOPLE WHO DIDN'T MOCK ME FOR IT!
IT'S WAY BIGGER THAN ME!
MY DREAM'S NOT JUST ABOUT ME!!
PLUS, THERE ARE THOSE WHO HAVE SUFFERED ...

I WANNA BE THE GUY TO SHOW THEM ALL A BRIGHT FUTURE!
THE SAME... ARE WE?

URGH!
THUD!
F
NG
ONCE I'M IN, I'LL DEACTIVATE THEIR SECURITY SYSTEM! THEN WE'RE FREE TO INFILTRATE!
HERE'S THE PC WITH THE PROGRAM I WHIPPED UP JUST FOR TODAY! THIS SPECIAL WIRELESS CONNECTION SHOULD GET ME ACCESS TO U.A.'S NETWORK, AND THEY'LL BE NONE THE WISER.
I BELIEVE! I BELIEVE IN YOU!!
NOT A SINGLE SOUL HAS YET TO PROVE THAT YOUR FEELINGS FOR ME ARE INADEQUATE!
FWIP
POP
THE BOTTOM OF THE HILL'S NOT CLOSE ENOUGH... CAN'T CONNECT.
THERE'S NO TIME TO LOSE!
YOU'RE GOING TO WIN!

I GOTTA GET CLOSER!
SHP
LA BRAVA!! IT'S TOO RISKY TO GO ALONE!
I GOTTA PLAY MY PART IN THIS!!
RUB
RUB
ALL FOR GENTLE'S SAKE!!
MY COMPANION WILL BE DEACTIVATING YOUR SCHOOL'S SENSORS.
SO...
...I HAVEN'T YET MEASURED UP TO THE FOES OF YOUR PAST?!
BOING
I MUST END THIS, FAST!!
GRAH

...DIGNITY, HONOR AND STYLE...
I SHALL ABANDON ALL NOTIONS OF...
...AND BRING YOU DOWN!
BWAM
BWAM
BWAM
BWAM
BWAM
BWAM
KER
WAAM
...YOU'VE PROVEN TO BE!
AS A SIGN OF RESPECT FOR THE MAN...

SKF
NO...
OH NO...!!

ST.
LOUIS
SHOOT
STYLE
...

GASP
...I'VE FOUGHT SO FAR, GENTLE.
THIS'S BEEN THE TOUGHEST BATTLE...
HUFF
UFF
SHP
FSSHH
SMASH !!

SOME HEROES'RE CLOSE BY!
TMP TMP TMP
RUSTIL
GENTLE!

THE LOVE-BASED POWER-UP IS A TEMPORARY ONE...

...AND IS LIMITED TO A SINGLE USE PER DAY.
PLEASE... JUST RUN.

NO... STOP IT!
PLIP
CLATTER
GET OFFA HIM!

I HAD HOPED TO SAVE YOUR QUIRK UNTIL OUR GRAND EXIT, YET...

GO AWAY!! STOP!!
BOP BOP BOP BOP BOP
GET OFFA MY GENTLE!
TOMP TOMP
SO GET OFF HIM! WHERE'S OUR BRIGHT FUTURE, HUH?!
BOP
HE DIDN'T EVEN STOP FOR HIS BELOVED TEA BREAKS WHILE PLANNING IT!
GENTLE PUT HIS HEART AND SOUL INTO THIS PLAN!
BOP
BOP
LA BRAVA...
HE'S MY EVERYTHING. YOU CAN'T STEAL HIM FROM ME!
GENTLE'S MY ONLY LIGHT IN THIS WORLD!!

BUT I KNEW FULL WELL YOU WOULD NEVER LEAVE ME BEHIND...
DIDN'T I JUST TELL YOU TO RUN AWAY?!
DON'T TAKE MY GENTLE AWAY!!
"PLEEEASE? I'M ALREADY A CRIMINAL, WHAT WITH ALL THE HACKING."
"NO, YOU MAY NOT ASSIST. THAT WOULD MAKE YOU AN ACCESSORY TO MY CRIMES."
"...I'LL BE HAPPY NO MATTER WHAT HAPPENS."
"BESIDES, AS LONG AS I'M WITH YOU, GENTLE..."
IF I CAN'T BE WITH GENTLE...
...I'LL JUST DIE!!
NO. I DARESAY SHE WOULD GO ON TO COMMIT CRIMES BEYOND ANYTHING WE'VE DONE SO FAR!
SHE WOULD NEVER BE HAPPY ESCAPING ON HER OWN.

LA BRAVA...
I MADE HER MY ACCOMPLICE!
I ACCEPTED HER HELP.
I LED HER TO THIS POINT.
RUSTL
RUSTL
RUSTL
RUSTL
...FOUND HAPPINESS!
I, TOO....
...THEY'LL SOON LEARN THAT LA BRAVA ASSISTED ME IN BATTLE.
SHE'S COMMITTED NO REAL SIN. YET, SHOULD THE HEROES CATCH US, LIKE THIS...!!
WOM
GUH
SO AT THE VERY LEAST...
SHP

WE CAN PRETEND THIS BATTLE NEVER HAPPENED!
FWIP
BWOP
ALL FOR HER. FOR HER BRIGHT FUTURE.
FSSHH
...TO LESSEN...
...HER CRIME.
IF ONLY...
TMP
NOW VANISH, IZUKU MIDORIYA.
WORMP

GENTLE CRIMINAL!
SKWEEZ
IT SEEMS I STUMBLED OVER A PEBBLE BY THE ROADSIDE.
U.A....
I SURRENDER.
TAKE PRIDE, IZUKU MIDORIYA. FOR YOU...
BOOM
...PROTECTED ALL THAT WAS. YOURS. THIS IS YOUR WIN.
G

CONGRATULATIONS ON VOLUME 20!!
AND THE MOVIE, AND FOUR YEARS OF SERIALIZATION!!
Congratulations on making it to 20 volumes, Horikoshi!
It feels like you went from a reprinting of volume 1 to an anime adaptation and megapopularity in the blink of an eye, and that Plus Ultra achievement makes me as happy as if it were my own!
As a devoted reader, I can't wait to see how the plot unfolds from here on out!
YOKO AKIYAMA
あきやま陽光

No. 181 - For Someone Else

U.A....
IN THE EVENT WE CONFIRM A HOSTILE PARTY...
NO. 181 - FOR SOMEONE ELSE
I SURRENDER.
...BE PREPARED TO CANCEL THE FESTIVAL AND EVACUATE ALL STUDENTS!

SURRENDER?
I RECOGNIZE HIM.
HE'S A VILLAIN WHO SPECIALIZES IN QUICK ESCAPES.
HE'S ALSO KNOWN FOR UPLOADING MISCHIEVOUS VIDEOS.
WHO'RE YOU WORKING WITH?
SHIP
GENTLE!
NO ONE.
WHAT'S WITH THE WOUNDS, HUH? AND THE TORN-UP FIELD?
AS I SAID, I TRIPPED AND FELL...!
JUST YOU TWO, THEN?
CORRECT.
CORRECT?! WHERE'S THE THIRD?
SNIFF
IT SMELLS LIKE ONE OF OUR STUDENTS!
NOW VANISH, IZUKU MIDORIYA.

FOR HER BRIGHT FUTURE.
ALL FOR HER.

...WHAT GENTLE CRIMINAL WAS DOING.
IT WAS THEN THAT I SOMEHOW UNDER-STOOD...

...JUST... OVER THERE...
HE SHOULD BE...

...UNTIL ALL THAT WAS LEFT IN ME, DEEP DOWN...
I FOUGHT WITH MY FEELINGS ON THE LINE...
SO, I'M OVER-JOYED THAT THIS WAS FOR YOU, IN THE END.
I'VE COMMITTED COUNTLESS CRIMES, BUT MY GREATEST SIN OF ALL WAS...

YET, ALL ALONG...
...I WAS DOING IT FOR ME.
I AM UTTERLY STRIPPED OF THE WILL TO FIGHT BACK.

I PUT A TASTEFUL SPIN ON MY SELFISH ACTIONS.

...THAT BEAT FOR SOME-ONE ELSE!
...ABDUCTING THIS POOR, NAIVE WOMAN...
...WAS A HEART...
...AND BRAIN-WASHING HER.

...TO PARDON MANAMI AIBA!
SO I ASK YOU NOW...

GENTLE ...!!
IT'S NOT RIGHT!
YOU'RE DOING THIS FOR ME?!

...WAS AGAINST YOU.
I'M GLAD THAT MY FINAL, CLIMACTIC CLASH...

YOUR INJURIES!

IZUKU MIDORIYA.

YOU KNOW THAT!
I NEVER WANTED TO MAKE TROUBLE FOR YOU, GENTLE.
IT'S NOT FAIR!
YOU FOUGHT THIS GUY?
I LOVE YOU WITH ALL MY HEART, GENTLE.

I FIGURED OUT THAT HE WAS GOING TO PRANK U.A.
SO YEAH... WE FOUGHT A LITTLE.

EVERY-THING'S OKAY NOW.

BUT ...

WAHHH!
AHHHHH!

SNIPE?
COME IN, HOUND DOG! ECTOPLASM C! RUSTLE UP ANYTHING STRANGE?
...
WE'RE WAITING FOR A REPORT, HERE.
KEEP EVERYONE ON ALERT, THOUGH.
TIG
CAN'T SAY I GET IT EITHER, BUT...
THE HECK ?
JUST SOME TROUBLEMAKER WHO UPLOADS PRANK VIDEOS. HE WANTS TO TURN HIMSELF IN.
...THERE'S NO EMERGENCY, FOR NOW.

IZUKU MIDORIYA ...
YOU'LL EXPLAIN YOURSELF IN DETAIL OVER AT THE POLICE STATION.
GENTLE CRIMINAL IS A MERE SHADOW OF A FAILED WOULD-BE HERO.
I, TOO, WAS ONCE ENROLLED IN A HERO COURSE.
THOUGH I AM IN NO POSITION TO GIVE ADVICE...
YOU'D STEAL A SMILE FROM A GIRL WHO DOESN'T KNOW THE MEANING OF JOY YET?!
THOSE FEELINGS OF YOURS—MAKE SURE TO SEE THEM THROUGH.

A BRIGHT FUTURE...?
HOW DID I END UP SO UTTERLY DISSATIS-FIED?
BECAUSE I WAS FECKLESS AND COWARDLY.

AH!
CLASS A'S PERFOR-MANCE STARTS AT TEN, RIGHT? IT'S 9:16 NOW... NO, 9:17.

ALL MIGHT WAS WORRIED ABOUT YOU.

GENTLE CRIMINAL...
WHERE? I'LL COME WITH YOU.
I'M SO SORRY, SENSEI, BUT I LEFT MY SHOPPING BAGS BACK THERE!
STILL...WE'LL BE BACK AT SCHOOL IN FIVE OR SIX MINUTES.

...WAS A TOUGH OPPONENT.

YEESH!
BOOO
WHY'S IT TAKING HIM THIS LONG TO DO A LITTLE SHOPPING?
HUH? WHERE'S MIDORIYA?
BANG 9:25 A.M.

I UNDERSTOOD WHY FIGHTING HIM WAS SO HARD FOR ME.
"A MERE SHADOW OF A FAILED WOULD-BE HERO."

IT WAS BECAUSE I MIGHT'VE TURNED OUT THAT WAY, TOO.
GENTLE AND I HAD SIMILAR FEELINGS.

WHILE I...
HIS FEELINGS CONCERNED LA BRAVA.

9:35 A.M.

HMPH!
KINDA PUMPED TO SEE IT.
WONDER HOW CLASS 1-A'S THING IS GONNA TURN OUT?

DEKU'S NOT GONNA DANCE?

THE MORONS'RE JUST LOOKING FORWARD TO WHAT WE'VE GOT FOR 'EM!
THEY'VE BEEN EXCITED SINCE THIS MORNING.
THERE'RE WAY MORE PEOPLE THAN I EXPECTED.

I SHOULD SAY SO...
A FINE TIME HE PICKED TO BLOW US OFF!!!
WHERE'S DEKU, AOYAMA?!
9:59 A.M.
SHOOM
OH!
OHH!
OH!
IT'S STARTING!
C'MON, FIRST-YEARS!!
HERE WE GO!
YAOYOROZU!!
CLAP
WOOOO
CLAP
CLAP

YEAHHH
WHAT'D THESE FIRST-YEARS COOK UP?!
YAOYOROZU!! YAOYOROZU!!
YAOYO-ROZU!
CLAP
CLAP
SHAH
LOOK, ERI!
SEE HIM ?!
YEAH...!
WHILE I...
LET'S DO THIS, DAMMIT!!

...JUST WANTED TO SEE YOU SMILE!

SUPER-DUPER WONDER COSTUMES WITH INCREASING/DECREASING BUTTON COUNTS

No. 182 - LET IT FLOW! SCHOOL FESTIVAL!
MIDORIYA! ☆ YOU'RE LATE!
AOYAMA!!
I'M SO SORRY!
WHY ON EARTH DO YOU LOOK SO BEAT UP?!
I TRIPPED...
YOU CLUMSY BOY! ☆
HERE! GET CHANGED! THE OTHERS ARE WAITING.
WAIT.
THANKS!
YOU'RE GOING ON-STAGE LIKE THAT? COVERED IN DIRT AND SCRATCHES?

GO CLEAN YOURSELF UP. THERE'S STILL TIME.
HOW WILL ANYONE ENJOY THE SHOW WHEN THEY'RE WORRIED ABOUT YOU?
GET BACK TO YOUR POST.
NOBODY ASKED YOU.
DOUBTS?! OVER WHAT?! I'M HYPED!
I...DON'T KNOW ABOUT THIS.
I JUST WANT A QUICK LOOKSEE!
SHIRKING PATROL DUTIES
CHAPERONING ERI
AND SOME BLAME THEIR FRUSTRATIONS ON CLASS 1-A.
THERE ARE MANY STUDENTS IN THE AUDIENCE IN OTHER DEPARTMENTS AND GRADES WHO AREN'T HAPPY WITH U.A.
THOSE MALCONTENTS AREN'T HERE TO HAVE FUN. THEY'RE HERE TO CRITICIZE THE PERFORMANCE.

I THINK IT'S FAIR TO SAY THEY'RE NOT HERE FOR THE ENTERTAINMENT.

BUT IT SEEMS LIKE THEY'RE JUST DOING IT FOR THEMSELVES.

A BAND? A DANCE SQUAD?
SURE... I BET THEY'LL PERFORM WELL.

LET'S DO THIS, DAMMIT!
WE'LL GRAB HOLD OF U.A. ...

KYOKA.
YOU SHOULD DO WHAT YOU WANT.

RIFF
BA
BAM
JA
...AND KILL 'EM WITH MUSIC !!
BOOM

DON
DOM
DON
WE GOTTA BE FLASHY TO HOOK 'EM!
WHAT AN EXPLOSIVE START!!

THANKS FOR COM-ING!
THIS AIN'T BAD !!
OH ?!
GOTTA MAKE IT GRIT-TIER!!

"...SO I WAS THINKING THIS MIGHT BE JUST THE THING TO CHEER HER UP!"
"SHE'S BEEN THROUGH SO MUCH..."
A SURPRISE? ERI'S GOING TO BE AT THE FESTIVAL?
...TO SHINE!
NOW IT'S TIME FOR AOYAMA AND MIDORIYA...
BAM
THEY'RE IN PERFECT SYNC...
MIDORIYA AND LASER BOY!
SHAH
HERE IT COMES !!
Oui! ☆
READY ?!

FLASH
FLING
A HUMAN FIRECRACKER!
HA HA HA HA
ALMOST TIME.
OOZE
GRITTER
CATCH!
Oof!
Oui!

US TOO!
DEKU!
...
IS THAT IT? JUST A SERIES OF PARLOR TRICKS?
AAAH
POP POP POP POP POP
HA HA HA HA
IT'S OVER?
THE BIG STUNT'S OVER? SO SHORT!!
BUT LOOK! OVER THERE!!
NOW, MY FEATHERED FRIENDS. MOVE THOSE LIGHTS UP, DOWN, SIDE TO SIDE!
HECK YEAH!
GO FOR IT, SERO-ROKI!!
FINISH FINISH FINISH
GOT IT!

WHAM WHAM
HERE'S THE HOOK, YOU DOOFS!
WHAM WHAM
WHAM
WHAM

KNOCK 'EM DEAD!

SHUP
WHO WANTS TO HAVE SOME FUN?!
PUT YOUR HANDS UP!
YEAHHHHH!
FLOAT
FLOAT
FLOAT
YEAHHHHH!
GET OUT THERE, DANCE SQUAD!!
Ready.
SHF
KAMINARI !!
DIAMOND DUST!!
CHK CHK CHK CHK
BWAHAHAHAHA...

FOR OUR FLOATING AUDIENCE MEMBERS— SOME TAPE TO KEEP YOU TIED DOWN AND SAFE!
SHP
MIDAIR GUITAR!
FLOAT
MY TIME HAS COME !!
SHFF
THAT DUDE'S STUCK DOING THE ROBOT!
KLANK
KLANK
YEAHHH!!
YEAH
I WANNA BE A HERO.
MOM. DAD.

SORRY ...
I'M NOT GONNA BE A MUSICIAN...
IT'S JUST THAT PUTTING MYSELF ON THE LINE TO FIGHT FOR OTHERS IS SO COOL!
YOU DON'T GET IT! I'VE BEEN STRUGGLING WITH THIS ALL ALONG!
RUB RUB
HEY! WHAT'S THERE TO CRY ABOUT?
AT FIRST, IT WAS JUST COOL AND FUN AND WE WERE GOOD AT IT.
BASIC STUFF LIKE THAT.
YOU SHOULD DO WHAT YOU WANT.
KYOKA.
YOUR MOM AND I WENT WITH MUSIC CUZ THAT'S WHAT WE LOVED.
I'VE ALWAYS ADMIRED WHAT YOU DO, MOM AND DAD... BUT NOW THE MUSIC YOU TAUGHT ME IS GONNA GO TO WASTE.
OUR FAMILY'S SO PASSIONATE ABOUT MUSIC... WHICH'S WHY I COULDN'T TELL YOU.

BUT THE LONGER WE PURSUED IT, THE MORE WE REALIZED...
...THE MUSIC WE MADE COULD ACTUALLY DO SOMETHING FOR OTHERS...
IN THAT SENSE...
...MUSIC AND HEROISM AREN'T SO DIFFERENT.

HYPOCRITE!
BAM
BAM

STOP SPEEDING UP THE TEMPO, DUMMY!
OF COURSE IT'S ALL GONNA FALL APART WHEN YOU START SHOW-BOATING!
HUH?
NO WEIRD AD-LIBBING TOMORROW, OKAY?

YEA

MIDORIYA!!
ARE YOU TWO WATCHING?
SIR NIGHTEYE!!

AH! MIDORIYA!!
SIR!!

YAYYYY
YEAHHHH !!
SHE'S REALLY SMILING !!
YEAHHH !!
SHE'S SMILING.

JUMP MAG VS. GRAPHIC NOVEL EDITION

Chapter 182.

This chapter was rough and sketchy when it came out in *Shonen Jump*, and I felt terrible about it. Especially for the readers who follow the story via the weekly chapters. Of all the chapters for this to happen… You couldn't even tell what was going on in some spots. It's all fixed up for this book, of course, and I've even added some additional bits and shifted things around to better fit my original vision.

Jiro's close-up gets a two-page spread, for one.

That's how I originally wanted to do it, so please think of this as an apology.

Still, I liked the version of Jiro I drew for the chapter in the magazine, so it's included below.

"You should do what you want." Thank you, Kyotoku (Jiro's dad).

NOW HEAR ME, COUNT PARIS, PHANTOM OF AZKABAN! I SHALL BE TAKING BACK MY JULIET!!
MY NAME IS ROMEO!!
NO. 183 - FESTIVAL ALL-DAY LONG!!
THAT HE WAS THE KING OF GONDOR... THAT WAS A LIE.
BUT, ROMEO... WHAT OBI-WAN TOLD YOU ABOUT YOUR FATHER...
BA-BA-AM
NOOOOOO!!
I AM YOUR FATHER!

YAP YAP
IT WAS KINDA FUNNY HOW THEY WERE SO INTO IT.
THAT WAS NUTS!
TALK ABOUT THE ULTIMATE CROSSOVER EVENT!!

THAT'S JUST HOW IT IS... WE GOTTA CLEAN UP THE MESS WE MADE!
YAP
YAP
WISH WE COULD'VE SEEN CLASS B'S PLAY.

I RAN OUT WITHOUT IT...
BUT AT LEAST PICK UP YOUR PHONE.
BEING LATE WASN'T THE ISSUE.

SOMEBODY'S IN TROUBLE!
YOU'LL BE SHOCKED.
CHECK YOUR MISSED CALLS...

GOOD JOB BACK THERE.
I GOT THE GIST OF IT FROM ECTO.
I'M SORRY FOR MAKING EVERYONE WORRY.
SHOOT
DON'T GO THINKING WHAT YOU DID WAS RIGHT!
YOU'RE STILL A STUDENT HERE, WITH ONLY A PROVISIONAL LICENSE!
BUT THAT DOESN'T MAKE IT OKAY!
PANT
THE SHOW DIDN'T GET CANCELED BECAUSE YOU WEREN'T HURT TOO BAD!
PANT
PANT
WE'RE HERE TO PROTECT YOU KIDS!
WHEN THERE'S A FIGHT, YOU RELY ON US!

HNF!
WHAM
THE FESTIVAL'S STILL ON, SO HAVE FUN, DAMMIT!!
RIGHT.
WIPE THAT GLOOMY LOOK OFF YOUR MUG AND GET GOING.
?!
THANK YOU, HOUND DOG.
PANT PANT
LOOK, ERI! MIDORIYA CAME FLYING AT US!
OH. YOU'RE HERE, DEKU.
THUD
YOU ONLY FORGET HOW TO TALK WHEN YOU'RE BARKING MAD...
WOOFWOOF
ROWF! GRRRR...
THRA
SH
YOU'RE RIGHT. I WAS CARELESS ...
HOWWWWL MIGHT!!

HEYYY, NICE SHOW!
From now on, you're known as "Errand Boy"...
...EVERYONE WAS DANCING AND JUMPING AROUND!
AT FIRST, THE BIG NOISES WERE SCARY, BUT THEN...
THAT ONE GIRL'S SINGING WAS REALLY INTENSE, AND...
AND IT GOT ALL COLD, LIKE "WHOOSH"!
AND THE LIGHTS WERE SPINNING EVERY-WHERE!
THEN THERE WAS A FLASHY LIGHT AND YOU DISAPPEARED, DEKU!
IT WAS AMAZING!

I'M SO GLAD YOU LIKED IT.
RUB
RUB
Carry these as well! ☆
AHH! SORRY, I'M HELPING! I'M HELPING!
YEAH? WELL, I WON'T BE GLAD IF WE'RE LATE! HELP OUT, SLACKER!
IT'S GREAT THAT IT WAS SO FUN.
YEAH...
...
WOW! THANKS A LOT!!
THAT WAS SICK! AND CRAZY FUN!
YO, CLASS A!!
YAP
YAP

WE WERE JUST HOPING YOU'D FAIL!!
SORRY, OKAY?!
INDEED!
THAT MEANS YOUR PLAN WORKED LIKE A CHARM, IDA!!
THEY MUST'VE BEEN STRESSED OUT, JUST LIKE SENSEI MENTIONED.
FLAWLESS VICTORY!
THEY REALLY DIDN'T HAVE TO TELL US THAT...
SCAMPER
WE GOT THE MESSAGE, LOUD AND CLEAR.
WE HEARD WHAT YOU WERE TRYING TO ACCOMPLISH WITH ALL THIS.
DON'T SWEAT IT.
IF ONLY WE COULD DO SOMETHING FOR THOSE WHO COULDN'T BE IN OUR AUDIENCE...
HOWEVER! WE ONLY GOT THROUGH TO THEM BECAUSE THEY CAME TO WATCH.

WE'LL DO OUR BEST TO HELP OTHERS HAVE A GOOD TIME, TOO.
THIS'LL BE OUR WAY OF PAYING YOUR MESSAGE FORWARD.
WHOA...
HA HA HA!
HA HA HA!
JUST CUT IT OUT! SERIOUSLY ...
THAT AIN'T SATISFYING... LET'S FIND WHOEVER DIDN'T WATCH AND DRAG 'EM OUT HERE!
THANK YOU FOR YOUR SUPPORT!
PRETTY GREAT, HUH?
...WE WON'T GET SEATS AT THE BEAUTY PAGEANT!
IF WE DON'T HURRY ...
OKAY, OKAY, SORRY! WHAT'S EATING YOU, MINETA?
GET BACK TO WORK!! WE GOTTA FINISH CLEANING UP THIS DUMB ICE!!
YEAH

KRAK
KRAK
HAHH !!
KENDO !!
WITH HER LOVELY DRESS, TORN TO SHREDS BY A MARTIAL ARTS DEMO, HER FANTASTIC PERFORMANCE COMBINES STRENGTH AND BEAUTY!!
WHAT A BREATH OF FRESH AIR!!
RR
MM
BB
HOW DULL!! THIS GIRL UNDERSTANDS NOTHING, AND SHE'LL NEVER MEASURE UP TO ME!!

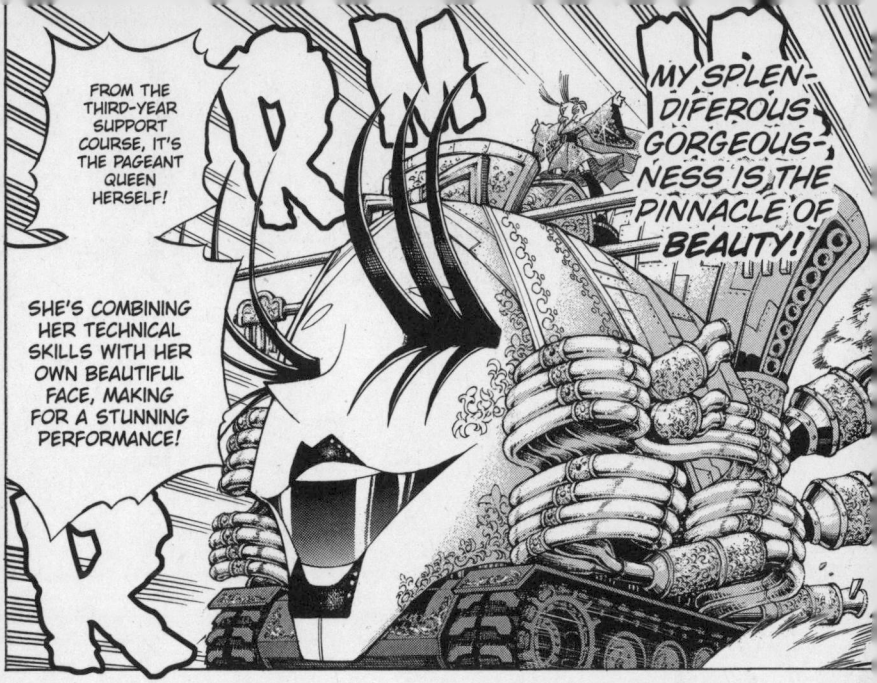
FROM THE THIRD-YEAR SUPPORT COURSE, IT'S THE PAGEANT QUEEN HERSELF!
MY SPLEN-DIFEROUS GORGEOUS-NESS IS THE PINNACLE OF BEAUTY!
SHE'S COMBINING HER TECHNICAL SKILLS WITH HER OWN BEAUTIFUL FACE, MAKING FOR A STUNNING PERFORMANCE!

CON-GRATS TO YOU GUYS, TOO!
HEY, I HEARD YOUR PLAY WENT OVER GREAT!
WHAM
HO HO! WELL DONE, THIRD-YEAR...

KLANK
KLANK
I WAS FOLLOWING A SECOND AGO, BUT NOW I'M LOST!
WHAT'S THIS SHOW ABOUT AGAIN?

C'MON, HADO... JUST REMEMBER, THE PEOPLE IN THE AUDIENCE ARE NOTHING BUT MAMMALS. YOU'LL BE FINE.
NEJIRE ...

FW
AH

TM
P

I LOST LAST YEAR BECAUSE...
...I TRIED TO MATCH KENRANZAKI'S FLASHINESS.
THAT'S KENRANZAKI'S SPECIALTY!
BUT I'VE...
...GOT OTHER THINGS GOING FOR ME!
URARAKA AND TSUYU...
SHE'S LIKE A PURE AND INNOCENT FAIRY...
WEIRD ...
TOGATA...
EVERYONE LOOKS SO SHOCKED!
WITH THAT LOOK... NOW THAT'S THE HADO WE KNOW!

SHE'S WON THE CROWD'S HEART! NEXT UP IS...
CLAP CLAP
YEAHHH
A DREAMY DANCE THROUGH THE SKY!
TMP

WHO SHOULD WE VOTE FOR?!
KENDO, FROM CLASS B! MAKE SURE SHE GETS ALL THE VOTES!!
LET'S VOTE!
SUBMIT YOUR VOTES NOW!! RESULTS WILL BE ANNOUNCED AT FIVE, AT THE FINAL EVENT!

CREPES, PLEASE!
THERE'RE SOME ATHLETIC EVENTS. WHO WANTS TO COMPETE?
COUNT ME OUT.
I'M IN!!
CLASS C'S HAUNTED LABYRINTH SOUNDS WILD. LET'S GO!!
SHUFFLE
I'M PUMPED FOR TONIGHT!

AFFL

結果発表！
出口
THANKS FOR COMING TODAY! WE HAD FUN, RIGHT?!
ERI, LOOK...
YEAH ...

SURPRISE!
FWIP

TMP
TMP
TMP
IT DIDN'T LOOK LIKE THERE'D BE ANY, BASED ON THE PROGRAM, SO...
THE CONVENIENCE STORE DIDN'T HAVE RED FOOD DYE, BUT SATO LENT ME SOME.
I PICKED UP THE INGREDIENTS WHEN I WENT SHOPPING. THEY'RE EASIER TO MAKE THAN I THOUGHT!

APPLES!
I BET THEY'LL HAVE CANDIED APPLES!

SOMEONE WAS SELLING THEM?! I LOOKED EVERY-WHERE!!
A CANDY APPLE!
Here, take one.

HEH...
EXTRA SWEET!

YOU'LL BE ABLE TO SEE THEM AGAIN SOON, I EXPECT.

NIP

I CAN ALWAYS MAKE MORE, SO LOOK FORWARD TO IT.
FLIK
FLIK
THROB
YES.
INCREDIBLE!
YOU TAUGHT YOURSELF TO DO ALL THIS?
WHOSH
AND YOU NEVER WANTED TO USE YOUR TALENTS TO DO GOOD IN THE WORLD?
I'M LA BRAVA.
WHAT DO YOU DO FOR A LIVING?
NEVER.

ALL I EVER WANTED WAS TO HELP GENTLE.

THERE'S A SIMPLE TEST TO TELL IF SHE'S REALLY BRAINWASHED OR NOT.
SO THAT IDIOTIC LIE WON'T FLY HERE.
SHE'S ACTUALLY JUST SMITTEN WITH YOU, YEAH?

HMPH ...
SO YOU LOVE HER TOO? YEESH...

SURE, PLENTY OF YOUR CRIMES WERE ONLY ATTEMPTED CRIMES, BUT THE SHEER NUMBER TELLS US SHE WAS IN ON IT.
AIBA NEVER TOOK PART DIRECTLY. MY CAPITAL OFFENSES ARE NOT HERS...

HIGH SCHOOL DROPOUT, HUH?
FORMERLY IN A HERO COURSE... BUT YOU WENT ASTRAY AND STARTED COMMITTING CRIMES ON VIDEO.

I RECALLED THE DREAM I ONCE HELD.
IT FRIGHTENED ME, AND I DASHED FORTH, HEADLONG.

DOWN THE WRONG PATH, PERHAPS...
WELL, GOOD THING YOU GAVE IT ALL UP TODAY.
THE ONLY PEOPLE WHO SAY THEY CAN'T TURN THEIR LIVES AROUND...
...ARE THE ONES WITH NO REAL DESIRE TO CHANGE.
THEY'RE TOO IMPATIENT. THEY WANT RESULTS RIGHT AWAY.
ANYWAY, WANT SOME TEA?
FINE BLACK TEA, IF YOU WOULD ...
WE ONLY GOT PLAIN OLD TEA...

HERO

YUYU HAYA [18]

THE UNIFORM

Birthday: 9/10
Height: 160 cm
Favorite Things: Everything cute

THE SUPPLEMENT

Nejire's good pal, who thinks Nejire is the cutest thing in the galaxy. Useless info: she dyes her hair, has piercings and generally does stylish stuff that wouldn't be allowed in real life.

AS NOVEMBER ENTERED ITS FINAL DAYS...
DING DONG
DING DONG
WHOOSH
NO. 184 - JAPANESE HERO BILLBOARD CHART
U.A. IS TAKING HER IN.
YOU WEREN'T KIDDING ABOUT HANGING OUT AGAIN SOON !!

WELL, IT'S NOT LIKE SHE CAN STAY IN THE HOSPITAL FOREVER.
SHE REMINDS ME OF MY LITTLE SISTER.
WOO-HOO, WE GOT OURSELVES AN ERI.
HOW'D THIS WORK OUT, EXACTLY ?!
HI, EVERY-BODY.

IN OTHER WORDS, SHE'S GOT NOWHERE TO CALL HOME.
SHE STILL HAS A GRANDFATHER, THE HASSAIKAI BOSS, BUT HE'S IN A COMA FOR THE FORESEEABLE FUTURE.
THEY SAY HER MOTHER ABANDONED HER.

FWIP FWIP

BUT IT'S STARTING TO GROW OUT, LITTLE BY LITTLE.

HER HORN IS THE SOURCE OF HER QUIRK.
PLUS, AIZAWA SENSEI MIGHT'VE MENTIONED THIS...
AND EVERYTHING SHOULD BE FINE WHILE IT'S ALL SHRUNKEN. WE HEARD...
Right.

ALL THE MORE REASON TO HAVE HER HERE WITH US INSTEAD OF AT AN ORPHANAGE.
NOD
HOLD ON... HOW DO WE KNOW THAT WON'T HAPPEN AGAIN?
THERE'LL ALSO BE REGULAR EXAMINATIONS... EVERYTHING... ONE STEP AT A TIME.
WE'LL OBSERVE HER AND TRY TO FIGURE OUT A WAY TO DEAL WITH HER INCREDIBLE POWER.
SHE'LL BE STAYING IN THE FACULTY DORM, WHERE I'LL KEEP AN EYE ON HER.
THAT'S WHERE I COME IN, SINCE I'M TAKING TIME OFF FROM SCHOOL! PLUS, ERI AND I ARE ALREADY PALS!
KERSHWING
THAT'S A BIG RESPONSIBILITY, AIZAWA SENSEI.
PAT
AND ONCE ERI'S BODY AND MIND HAVE STABILIZED...
OF COURSE!
I KNOW YOU ALL HAVE BUSY LIVES, BUT STOP BY EVERY ONCE IN A WHILE.

I ADMIT, THAT WOULD BE NICE!
HA HA HA!

IT WON'T BE LONG UNTIL OUR INVINCIBLE DUDE MAKES A COMEBACK.

YOU'RE EXPECTING GUESTS.
NO. BACK TO THE DORMS, WITH THE REST OF CLASS A.

CAN WE PLAY TOO?
ROGER THAT. WE'LL PLAY OTHELLO OR SOME-THING!
IT'S SHORT NOTICE, BUT COULD YOU THIRD-YEARS WATCH HER FOR A BIT?

JOLT
ACHOO!

1-A
ALLIANCE

LIKE WHOEVER WAS SHOUTING "YAOYOROZU!"
OR MAYBE YOU HAVE SOME FANS WHO'RE GOSSIPING ABOUT YOU?!
PLEASE DON'T TEASE ME. I'M JUST HAPPY TO HAVE AN ADMIRER!
NO... I'M IN PERFECT HEALTH, AND MY MUCUS MEMBRANES ARE FUNCTIONING PROPERLY.
ARE YOU FEELING SICK?
UH...
YOU PROBABLY ALREADY HAVE A TON OF FANS, TOKOYAMI.
ESPECIALLY AFTER DOING YOUR WORK STUDY WITH HAWKS.
AH!!
THEY'RE HERE, EVERYONE! LET'S GREET THEM!!
KLIK
THAT ALL WENT A BIT TOO QUICKLY.
NO, I DON'T THINK SO.

STINGINGLY CUTE AND CATLIKE!
We've come from... somewhere...
WE'VE COME TO LEND A PAW AND HELP!!
ROCK ON WITH THESE SPARKLING GAZES!
PAW PAD MANJU
WILD, WILD...
...PUSSY-CATS!
(DAY-OFF VERSION)

I HOPE MY LITTLE KITTIES HAVE ALL BEEN WELL!
YAYYYY
PUSSYCATS! IT'S GREAT TO SEE YOU AFTER ALL THIS TIME!
PAW PAD MANJU!
PAW PAD MANJU!
WE'RE DOING GOOD, THANKS.
DON'T REMIND ME...
LOOM
SORRY WE COULDN'T PROTECT YOU, BACK THEN.
SURE...
UH-HUH.
THANKS FOR THAT LETTER! IT MEANT A LOT, REALLY!
KOTA!! LONG TIME NO SEE!!
BAM
HUH?
C-CUT IT OUT.
LOOK HERE, MIDORIYA.

NOW WE MATCH!
HE PICKED THEM HIMSELF. "THEY HAVE TO BE RED," HE SAID.
YOU'VE... GOT IT WRONG...
SO WHY ARE YOU HERE AT U.A.?
WE'RE JUST HERE TO ANNOUNCE THAT WE'RE BACK.
We've gotta go see class B anyway!
Oh, don't trouble yourselves.
FWIP FWIP
Please, have a seat.
JUST CALL ME THE CAT-MINISTRATIVE ASSIS-TANT!
NOT BACK IN ACTION PER SE, BUT I'LL BE IN THE AGENCY, SUPPORTING THE OTHER THREE!
SHWIP SHWIP
CONGRAT-ULATIONS!!
YOU'RE BACK ?!
WITH YOUR QUIRK STOLEN, I THOUGHT YOU HAD TO QUIT?
YOU TOO, RAG-DOLL?

WHEN I SEE A GOOD QUIRK, I JUST NEED TO HAVE IT.
IT'S NOT RIGHT, I KNOW.
WE DID HEAR FROM HIM, IN TARTARUS...
DEFINITELY A BAD HABIT OF MINE.
I'D LOVE TO RETURN HERS, BUT THAT WOULD INVOLVE USING MY OWN QUIRK.

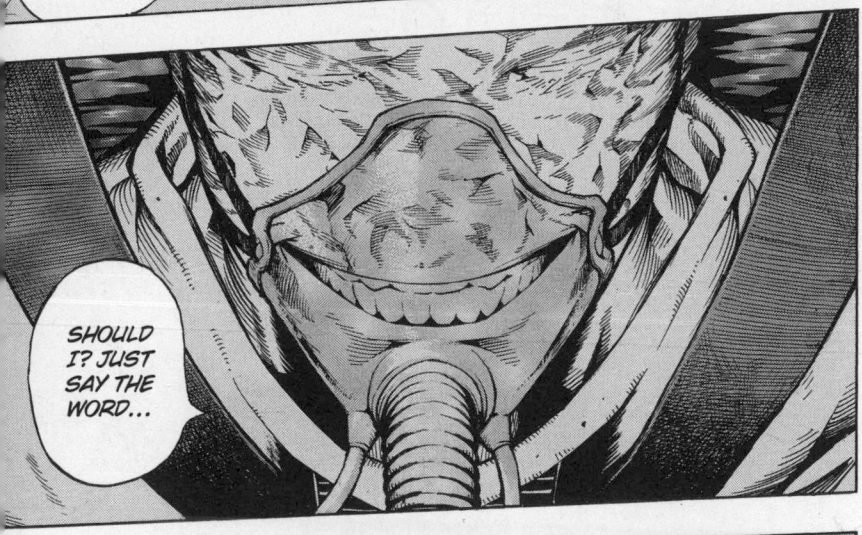
SHOULD I? JUST SAY THE WORD...

THEN WHY RETURN NOW?

SO IN THE MEANTIME, KEEPING HIM COMPLETELY IMMOBILIZED IS THE SAFEST OPTION.
THEY'RE STILL PRESSING HIM TO FIND OUT WHAT KINDS OF QUIRKS HE'S GOT LOCKED UP INSIDE HIM, AND HOW MANY.

BECAUSE THEY'RE ABOUT TO ANNOUNCE...
...THIS YEAR'S SECOND JAPANESE HERO BILLBOARD CHART.
WE'RE IN 411TH PLACE.
JAPANESE HERO BILLBOARD CHART!!
INCIDENT RESOLUTION RATE, CONTRIBUTIONS TO SOCIETY, PUBLIC APPROVAL RATING...
ALL THESE FACTORS MATTER WHEN DETERMINING THE OFFICIAL HERO RANKINGS TWICE A YEAR!!
THE ONES WHO REACH THOSE UPPER ECHELONS OF HEROISM...
...ARE HEROES WHO PRESERVE THE PEACE AND KEEP THE PUBLIC SMILING!!

WHY DO YOU THINK WE'RE STILL IN THE TRIPLE DIGITS, DESPITE ZERO ACTION?!
WRONG, MEOW!
OH! SO YOU'RE DOING THIS TO STOP YOUR SHARP DECLINE!!
BUT YOUR TEAM WAS 32ND LAST TIME!
BAM
WHICH MEANS PEOPLE ARE COUNTING ON US...
OUR APPROVAL RATING, AT LEAST, WAS AS HIGH AS EVER.
...SO WE CAN'T STOP MOVING FORWARD!!
NOT WITH ALL THAT'S BEEN HAPPENING.
OH YEAH. THEY HAVEN'T ANNOUNCED THIS YEAR'S SECOND RANKINGS YET.
THE BILLBOARD CHART, RIGHT...
I HEAR YOU! THE WILD, WILD PUSSYCATS ARE DUDES AMONG DUDES!!
Pipe down.
SNIFFLE

IT'S THE FIRST BILLBOARD CHART SINCE THE KAMINO INCIDENT!!
AND EVERYONE EVERYWHERE UNDERSTANDS HOW MAJOR THIS IS!!
BILLBOARD CHARTS

NEVER BEFORE HAVE HEROES TAKEN THE STAGE IN PERSON AT THIS PRESENTATION.
THE TIMES, HOWEVER, ARE A-CHANGING! STAY TUNED!!

A BILLBOARD CHART WITHOUT ALL MIGHT, HUH?
CAN'T WAIT TO FIND OUT. SHOULD BE EXCITING!

NO. 10!
SHE USED TO BE NINTH, BUT SHE FELL A SPOT!!
I'M HONESTLY NOT SURE I DESERVE THIS...
DRAGON HERO: RYUKYU!!
NO. 9!
ANOTHER ONE WHO FELL! THAT'S UNPRECEDENTED FOR HIM!!
HMPH...
THE TOP THREE ASIDE, IT'S JUST LUCK AND TIMING...
...THAT DETERMINE THE REST OF THE RANKINGS.
EQUIPPED HERO: YOROI MUSHA!
NO. 8!
YOU KNOW HIM FROM THOSE "CLEAN 'N' SHINY" COMMERCIALS ...
LAUNDRY HERO: WASH!
WASHASHASHA-SHASHA!!

NO. 7!

IT'S A GREAT LEAP FORWARD FOR THIS UP-AND-COMER!!

WHAT AN HONOR.

KAMUI WOODS!

NO. 4!
THE MYSTERIOUS SHINOBI WHOSE INCIDENT RESOLUTION RATE AND SUPPORT ARE SKYROCKETING...
NINJA HERO: EDGE-SHOT!
KEEP QUIET. WE'RE IN PUBLIC.
NO. 5!
THIS UNYIELDING BUNNY WAS BUMPED UP IN THE RANKINGS!
ONLY WEAKLINGS JOIN TEAMS!
RABBIT HERO: MIRKO!
WITH A HIGHER PUBLIC SUPPORT RATE THAN ANYONE, IT'S THE FIBER HERO!
STILL AT NO. 3, EVEN THOUGH HE'S TAKING TIME OFF!
WHICH BRINGS US TO THE NEXT MAN!!
IT SEEMS ANY HERO INVOLVED WITH WHAT HAPPENED IN KAMINO HAS SEEN HIS OR HER FORTUNES RISE!

HE DOES THINGS HIS WAY, BUT ALWAYS FIERCELY! WITH UNSTOPPABLE MOMENTUM, HE'S MADE IT TO SECOND PLACE!
NO. 2!
ABSENT
BEST JEANIST!
LAYING IT ON THICK, HUH?
WING HERO: HAWKS!
EVERYONE'S ANXIOUSLY AWAITING HIS SWIFT RETURN!!
HE'S WAITED A LONG TIME TO CLAIM THE THRONE AND BECOME...
AND FINALLY!! THIS GUY'S BEEN ON TOP FOR A LITTLE WHILE NOW, BUT TODAY IT'S OFFICIAL!

FLAME HERO: ENDEAVOR !!
NO. 1!!

WHAT ARE YOU?!

This guy is absurdly popular with little kids. I like him.

JAPANESE HERO BILLBOARD CHART

The Heroes Public Safety Commission looks over the past year of heroism and—after using a proprietary formula to quantify incident resolution rate, societal contributions and public approval rating—presents the results in the form of rankings.

Because incident resolution rate is the most important factor and heroes who tackle bigger incidents end up with even more public support, those involved in major crises quickly find themselves climbing the ranks.

...BECAUSE THIS IS A CRITICIAL JUNCTURE FOR OUR TIMES.
PRESIDENT OF THE HEROES PUBLIC SAFETY COMMISSION
WE DECIDED TO PUT ON SUCH AN ELABORATE CEREMONY...
DUNNN
AND WORD ON THE STREET IS THAT OUR SOCIETY IS STILL MISSING AN ICON...
IT'S BEEN ABOUT THREE MONTHS SINCE ALL MIGHT'S RETIREMENT.
GLARE
SO LET US JOIN THEM IN THEIR QUEST FOR A PEACEFUL SOCIETY.
BUT THE HEROES STANDING BEFORE YOU ARE READY TO TAKE ON THE MANTLE.
PSST
HOW'S IT FEEL TO BE ON TOP?

THANK YOU FOR THIS HONOR.
HOW-EVER ...
IN TRUTH, I WOULD'VE WITHDRAWN MY NAME IF THAT WERE ALLOWED.
AND NOW, A WORD FROM OUR HEROES!
...
RYUKYU!
...SO GOING FORWARD, I'LL STRIVE TO REALLY EARN MY RANKING.
THERE HAVE BEEN LIVES I COULDN'T SAVE...
WAIT YOUR TURN, CRUST...
WE CAN DO IT, RYUKYU!! I BELIEVE IN US!!
THAT'S NOT A BAD THING, I GUESS...
HE'S A LITTLE INTENSE.
THAT PAIN IN YOUR HEART! LIKE YOU'RE JUST NOT GOOD ENOUGH!!
I FEEL YOU, RYUKYU!
WE NEED TO STAND TALL AND FIGHT ON!!

WASHA !!
THE MISSION IS THE SAME AS EVER.
...SO I'D LIKE TO MAKE HIM AND ALL MY SUPERIORS PROUD.
EDGESHOT WAS KIND ENOUGH TO LET ME JOIN HIS TEAM...
...
IT STILL HURTS DEEP DOWN EVERY TIME I THINK ABOUT IT!!
ARGHHHH
WHY WASN'T I IN KAMINO THAT DAY ?!
HOPE YOU'RE READY FOR ME TO KICK YOUR BUTTS.
TO ALL THE PLOTTERS AND SCHEMERS OUT THERE!!

NUMBERS DON'T CONCERN ME.
IF PUBLIC APPROVAL WERE THE ONLY FACTOR, YOU'D BE IN THIRD PLACE!
...BUT I DON'T DO THIS JOB FOR FAME OR REPUTATION.
SWING
I'M GRATEFUL TO ALL MY SUPPORTERS, OF COURSE...
THE ABILITY TO PRESERVE LAW AND ORDER IS THE TRUE MEASURE OF A HERO.
WHO THE HECK DO YOU THINK WANTS TO HEAR THAT CRAP?!
People like Stain, yeah?

SHAR

Ahh!
SHP
I JUST HATE HOLDING BACK HOW I FEEL.

YOU ALWAYS DID ENJOY ROCKING THE BOAT.
SASSY. I LIKE IT!

I'D BE SECOND, EDGESHOT'D BE THIRD...
ENDEAVOR, FOURTH, AND SO ON.

F
AHEM...
WAP
BEST JEANIST WOULD BE NUMBER ONE IF THAT WAS ALL THAT MATTERED, THANKS TO THE BOOST HE'S GOTTEN DURING HIS LEAVE OF ABSENCE.
YOU WANNA TALK PUBLIC SUP-PORT?

SURE... IT MATTERS MORE THAN ANYTHING ELSE NOW, BUT C'MON...
PUBLIC APPROVAL?

FW
OUR SYMBOL'S GONE.
AND YOU SAY THAT STAYING THE COURSE IS THE ANSWER?
THIS ISN'T THE TIME TO DWELL ON THE PAST.
FWAP
TODAY'S A TURNING POINT, SO WHAT I DON'T WANNA HEAR...
...IS A BUNCH OF P.R.-FRIENDLY SOUND BITES FROM THE GUYS AND GALS BELOW ME!
TRY COMING UP WITH SOMETHING ACTUALLY HEROIC TO SAY!
FWAP
...BUT NOW I'VE GOT NO CLUE WHAT THIS GUY'S THINKING...
CHATTER
IT LOOKED LIKE HE WAS BEING GROUCHY A SECOND AGO...

HAWKS, AGE 22.
A HERO WHO BROKE INTO THE TOP THREE DURING THE LAST RANKING.
HE STARTED HIS OWN AGENCY AT JUST 18...
...AND MADE IT INTO THE TOP TEN OF THAT YEAR'S SECOND RANKING.

THE WORLD'S FIRST EVER TO MAKE TOP TEN AS A TEEN-AGER.
PEOPLE SAY HE DOES THINGS A LITTLE TOO FAST!
THAT FAST, THAT YOUNG!!

CHATTER
CHATTER

ARROGANT JERK.
TALK ABOUT DOING THINGS AT YER OWN PACE...

FWOOSH
THAT'S ALL FROM ME.
YOU'RE NEXT.
DUDE WITH A LOWER APPROVAL RATING THAN ME...
MR. NUMBER ONE.
SHP
FWIP
IT'S HARD TO ARGUE AGAINST WHAT HAWKS SAID.
HE'S A TOUGH ACT FOR ENDEAVOR TO FOLLOW...

AFTER MY JUNIOR COLLEAGUE FANNED THE FLAMES LIKE THAT...

SH
I DON'T HAVE MUCH TO SAY.
P

WHAT PURPOSE DOES OUR STRENGTH SERVE?
THE ANSWER IS A SIMPLE ONE.

SO, #1 HERO...
WHAT'S IT MEAN TO BE THE SYMBOL OF PEACE?

EXCEPT... JUST WATCH ME!

CLAP
CLAP

ENDEAVOR

EXPLAIN YOURSELF, KID!
GUOOOM
SHZZ
SHZZ
YIKES! SORRY FOR PUTTING YOU ON THE SPOT THERE!

NO WAY! MORE LIKE ASSISTING!
SHUP
IT DID THE TRICK, RIGHT?

TESTING ME, HUH?

...THOUGHT WE NEEDED TO SHAKE THINGS UP.
EVERYONE WAS JUST RATTLING OFF THE USUAL LINES, SO I...
Hot, hot.
SHZZ
SHZZ

BUT EVEN SO, HIM STEPPING DOWN CAME AS A SHOCK TO ME.
I NEVER WANTED TO BE LIKE HIM.
I WASN'T A BIG FAN OF ALL MIGHT.

SO THANKS FOR THE REASSURANCE! YOU WERE COOL OUT THERE.
YOU'LL NEVER BE IDOLIZED. NOT THE WAY HE WAS.
STILL ...
THERE'S NO DENYING THAT WE SERIOUSLY NEED A NEW LEADER NOW.
I HATE GUYS LIKE YOU THE MOST.
WE'RE DONE HERE. GO MAKE THE ROUNDS AND APOLOGIZE TO THE OTHERS.
I WISH I WAS LOWER DOWN. THERE'S MORE FREEDOM THERE!
Between 20th and 30th place.
DO I LOOK LIKE THE TYPE TO YOU?
HA HA HA HA!
IS THIS FOOL SERIOUS? OR MOCKING ME?
AND YOU NEVER WANTED TO TAKE ON THAT ROLE YOURSELF?

*SIGN: HIDAMARI KINDERGARTEN

HIGH-END!
WON'T LET YOU DOWN...
SKL
IT
W-W-WON'T... L-LET...

NO. 186 - ENDEAVOR AND HAWKS

STAFF INTRODUCTION

POCCHARI
(IKEDA-KUN)

Horikoshi's comment: What a cool character!

F-29
(FUSHIMI-KUN)

Horikoshi's comment: What a cool character!

IN CHANT MANAGER
(SAKAINO-KUN)

Horikoshi's comment: What a cool character!

PAPA RUSH
(NOGUCHI-KUN)

Horikoshi's comment: What a cool character!

HISTORY-EYE
(YUZAWA-KUN)

Horikoshi's comment: What a cool character!

YORITOMISAN
(YORITOMI-SAN)

Horikoshi's comment: What a cool character!

THREE YEARS I GAVE TO THIS COMPANY, BUT TODAY I'M TAKING IT DOWN.
MUTTER
MUTTER

YOU WORTHLESS COMPANY ...
ONCE YOU'RE GOOD AND GONE...
LIBERATION.
LIBERATION.
BUT TODAY, MY TALE COMES TO AN END.

IT'S BEEN SUFFOCATING.
FROM AS FAR BACK AS I CAN REMEMBER, I'VE LIVED MY LIFE AS A BOOTLICKER.
UNPRECEDENTED REPRINT OF DESTRO'S LIFE STORY

FLAD
LONG LIVE ...
... META-HUMAN LIBERATION!!
TERUO HAZUKASHI (AGE 31)
QUIRK: SHAME
THE MORE EMBARRASSED HE IS, THE STRONGER HE GETS.

WHAM WHAM
SO WHAT'RE YOU IN THE MOOD TO EAT, ENDEAVOR?
WHAM WHAM

YOU'RE HUNGRY, YEAH?
I KNOW A GREAT HOT POT PLACE WITH GOOD CHICKEN STOCK.
GAB
PRETTY BRAVE ON SUCH A COLD DAY.
WHOA, CHECK IT OUT!! WE'VE GOT A FLASHER.
FEATHERS? IT MUST BE...
KYAA
GAB

COME BACK, SCHWARTZ!!
AHH!
My little Schwartz, thank goodness.
OR A YAKITORI JOINT! THIS PLACE CALLED YORITOMI HAS AMAZING LIVER SKEWERS.
SHWIP
...
SHWIP
FWAH
OH, LET ME CARRY THAT UP FOR YOU, MA'AM.
HEYA.
THANK YOU.
FLOAT
HEY, IT'S HAWKS !!
YOU DON'T OFTEN SEE HIM JUST WALKING AROUND!

EXCUSE ME!
COULD MY SON HAVE YOUR AUTOGRAPH? HE'S A BIG FAN.
YO.
HAWKS, HAWKS!
ENEMIES?
WE CAUGHT THE SHOW YESTERDAY! KEEP UP THAT ARROGANT ACT AND YOU'RE GONNA MAKE MORE ENEMIES!
CONGRATS ON SECOND PLACE, HAWKS!

HIS PRESENCE... IT'S KINDA INTIMIDATING ...
THAT GUY'S GOT A MEAN FACE.
THERE'S ENDEAVOR ...!
CHATTER
CHATTER

HERE YOU GO, RYOSUKE. THANKS FOR BEING A FAN.
RYOSUKE!
WHAT'S YOUR NAME, KID?
OF COURSE!
ON A SWELL BACKPACK LIKE THIS? SURE YOU WANT ME WRITING ON IT?
TOUCH TOUCH
YAY

I DO! BUT IT'D JUST BE WRONG!!
BUT YOU SAID YOU LIKED HIM!
NO WAY.
HEY. GO GET HIS AUTO-GRAPH.

CRAP CRAP CRAP! THAT NEW COSTUME'S JUST TOO COOL!
WHA-?! WHA-?! WHY?!
HE'S COMING THIS WAY!
ACK!
THR
UST

DON'T LET ME SCARE YOU OFF NOW.

WRONG? HOW?!
THIS IS WRONG.

THIS IS WRONG?
It worked just fine with that buzz-cut guy from Shiketsu...

ENDEAVOR'S CHANGED!! FOR THE WORSE!!
WAAAH

THE ENDEAVOR I KNOW DOESN'T DO THIS KINDA STUFF FOR FANS!! HE'S TOO COOL TO STOOP TO THAT LEVEL!
SHAKA
SO SERIOUS ABOUT IT...
*FAN SERVICE

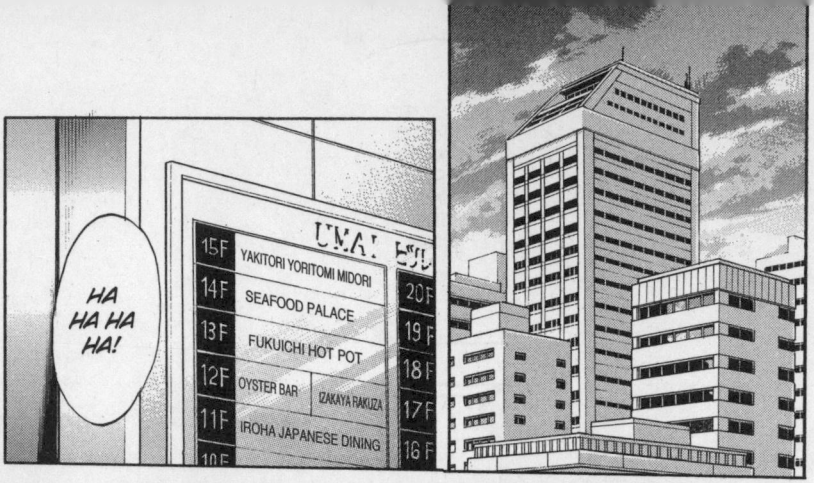
HA HA HA HA!
15F YAKITORI YORITOMI MIDORI
14F SEAFOOD PALACE
13F FUKUICHI HOT POT
12F OYSTER BAR
IZAKAYA RAKUZA
11F IROHA JAPANESE DINING
20F
19F
18F
17F
16F

YOU GLUTTON.
OH. ARE YOU GONNA FINISH THAT?
IT'S JUST NOT IN YOUR CHARACTER.
THAT'S WHAT THEY'LL TELL YOU, YEAH ...
Go on. Eat your fill.

MUNCH
MUNCH
MUNCH
LIKE AFTER THE SPORTS FESTIVAL, WHEN I TRIED SCOUTING YOUR BOY.
THE SON OF NUMBER TWO WOULD'VE BEEN A NICE FEATHER IN MY CAP.
A good attention grabber.

THAT'S HOW I AM. WHEN I WANT SOMETHING, I GO FOR IT.

FLARE
YOU'RE NO U.A. ALUM, BUT YOU SURE STAY INFORMED.
SINCE LITTLE SHOTO TARNISHED HIS REP BY FAILING HIS LICENSING EXAM.
BUT NOW I'M GLAD IT WAS TSUKUYOMI WHO CAME TO ME.
*TSUKUYOMI IS TOKOYAMI'S HERO NAME!
WHY'D YOU REALLY DRAG ME DOWN TO KYUSHU?
CUT THE CRAP.
FWIP FWIP
I KEEP MY EYES AND EARS OPEN.
THE RUMORS?
GET TO THE POINT ALREADY.
THE LEAGUE'S FREAKY REMODELED PUPPETS.
THOSE NOMU...

THE LEAGUE'S MADE SOME TROUBLE SINCE THEN, BUT THERE HAVEN'T BEEN ANY MORE NOMU SIGHTINGS.
WHEN WE CAPTURED ALL FOR ONE, WE ALSO FOUND A FEW DOZEN THAT WERE STASHED AWAY IN KAMINO.
SO YOU MUST HAVE PROOF IF YOU'RE SUGGESTING TEAMING UP...
YOU'RE THE ONE TALKING RUMORS.
THOSE ARE THE TWO LINES OF THOUGHT.
...OR THERE'S MORE, BUT ONLY OLD A.F.O. KNOWS WHERE THEY ARE.
SO EITHER YOU ROUNDED UP ALL OF THEM...
THE NOMU SIGHTINGS AREN'T JUST HAPPENING HERE.
HOLD ON, NOW. LISTEN.
OR HAVEN'T YOU HEARD?
CHECK! I'M OUT OF HERE!
FLARE
NOPE, NO PROOF. JUST RUMORS.

I FIRST HEARD ABOUT IT FROM THE LOCALS WHEN I WAS AWAY ON BUSINESS.

SO I TEAMED UP WITH THE POLICE, THOUGH WE KEPT THE INVESTIGATION UNDER WRAPS TO AVOID PANIC. NOTHING TURNED UP.

THOSE REMODELED VILLAINS ARE JUST ABOUT THE CREEPIEST THINGS ON PEOPLE'S MINDS, RIGHT?
...THE SYMBOL...
THEY TOOK DOWN THE FLAG!
?!
AFTER U.A., HOSU CITY AND KAMINO...
NOW, I'M TALKING PURELY HYPO-THETICAL, BUT...

AND NOW THOSE TALES ARE SPREADING ACROSS THE COUNTRY.
BUT I SAY SOME IDIOT GOT IT IN THEIR HEAD TO TELL A FEW TALES AND RILE PEOPLE UP.

THEY REPUBLISHED SOME OLD-SCHOOL CRIMINAL'S AUTOBIOGRAPHY, AND IT'S FLYING OFF THE SHELVES.
THIS IS KINDA LIKE THAT.
THAT GUY EARLIER, SCREAMING "LONG LIVE METAHUMAN LIBERATION" ...
I'M THINKING THAT'S INFLUENCING PEOPLE.
SLAP
META-HUMAN LIBER-ATION!
LONG LIVE ...

WHAT'RE YOU GETTING AT, HERE? SPIT IT OUT.
GRR
GRR
WELL AIN'T YOU A KNOW-IT-ALL.
THAT STUFF TENDS TO SELL BEST WHEN SOCIETY'S FEELING UNSTABLE, RIGHT?
PUFF OUT YOUR CHEST AND GIVE THEM THE MESSAGE!
WHILE I SIT BACK AND TAKE IT EASY!
I WANT OUR TOP HERO TO BE A LEADER WE CAN RELY ON!
...AND TELL EVERY-ONE THERE'S NOTHING TO FEAR!
YOU SHOULD BE THE ONE TO LOOK INTO THESE OMINOUS RUMORS ...
DO SOME LEISURELY PATROLLING, PUT IN A FEW APPEARANCES ...
...SAY "AW SHUCKS, NO TROUBLE TODAY" AND GET A GOOD NIGHT'S SLEEP! THAT'S MY IDEAL LIFE!
SERIOUSLY.
I JUST WANNA ENJOY MYSELF.
THIS IS YOUR SHOW TO DIRECT, MR. NUMBER ONE.
LIKE I BASICALLY SAID YESTERDAY ...
WHAT KINDA STANCE IS THAT?

I WANNA MAKE THIS WORLD ONE WHERE HEROES HAVE TIME TO KILL.

UM. ENDEAVOR.

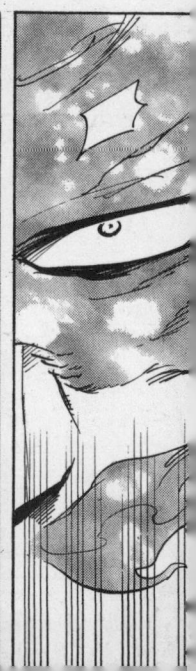

OM
100
YOUR BILL, GENTLE-MEN.
...
FWOO
GET BACK, MISS!

CRASH
WHO'S THE BEST HERE?
THE STRON-GEST?

HAWKS, GET HER TO SAFETY!
ROGER THAT! AND YOU, ENDEAVOR ?
EEEEEEEEK!
SHP
SKLURP
HERE WE GO.
IT'S YOUR LUCKY DAY, PAL.
OOM
SHT
SOME RUMORS ARE TRUE, HUH?
BURST

CUZ I CAME LOOKING FOR A FIGHT!
LUNGE
JET BURN!!

YOU WANT NUMBER ONE? YOU GOT HIM!
C'MON!
FLASH-FIRE FIST...

HERO

MIRKO [26] [RUMI USAGIYAMA]

STREET CLOTHES

Birthday: 3/1
Height: 159 cm
Favorite Thing: Carrots

THE SUPPLEMENT

Designwise, she's an amalgamation of my likes and preferences.

Her hero name is a reference to a certain MMA fighter.

THANKS, AS ALWAYS!
I'LL LEAVE YOUR CLEAN LAUNDRY OVER HERE, MOM.
NO. 187 - FLAMING ROAR! VS. NOMU: HIGH-END
NATSUO TODOROKI (19) SHOTO'S BROTHER
WE DON'T DO SO WELL WITH HEAT.
GOOD. I LIKE THE COLD, YOU KNOW.
FUYUMI TODOROKI (22) SHOTO'S SISTER
IT'S SUPPOSED TO GET REALLY COLD NEXT WEEK.
YOU'RE LOOKING WELL, NATSU.
REI TODOROKI SHOTO'S MOTHER
LOOKS NICE AND HEALTHY !!
YOUR COM-PLEXION ...
A-ANYWAY, YOU'RE LOOKING GOOD TOO, MOM!
I CALL HOME NOW AND THEN. AIN'T THAT ENOUGH?!
SIS!!
DID YOU FIND YOURSELF A GIRLFRIEND IN ONE OF YOUR SEMINARS?
WE DON'T SEE YOU MUCH, EVER SINCE YOU STARTED COLLEGE.
Yikes!

HE'S STRUGGLING WITH THE EXTRA LICENSE TRAINING...
...BUT HE'S WORKING HARD TO KEEP UP WITH HIS FRIENDS.
FWIP
YES, SHOTO'S BEEN SENDING ME LETTERS.

I SUPPOSE THAT'S UP TO MY DOCTOR...
Writing actual letters is rough.
CAN'T THEY JUST LET YOU HAVE A CELL PHONE ALREADY?
SHWIP

BECAUSE OF TRAINING AND THE DORM SYSTEM, HE CAN'T STOP BY AS MUCH ANYMORE.
I DIDN'T THINK SHOTO WAS THE TYPE TO WRITE HOME.
OHH?
FWIP

MOM.

THEY MADE HIM NUMBER ONE YESTERDAY. IT'S OFFICIAL.
ABOUT HIM...

NATSU.
THE WORLD STILL DOESN'T KNOW THE TRUTH ABOUT YOU. ABOUT OUR SIBLINGS...
ABOUT HOW HE'S ALWAYS TREATED HIS FAMILY.
FOR ONE, HE DOESN'T DO THE TALK SHOW CIRCUIT.
WHY'D YOU HAVE TO BRING UP DAD?
IT'S FINE, FUYUMI.
I CAN BARELY REMEMBER MOST OF IT, REALLY.
THINKING BACK, HE WAS LIKE A PERFECT STRANGER.
BUT ...
WHAT HE DID TO YOU, TO SHOTO AND TO... WELL, I CAN'T LET ANYONE PRETEND IT ALL NEVER HAPPENED...
IT'S BEEN ALMOST TEN YEARS.
AND HE STILL HASN'T COME TO APOLOGIZE TO YOU.
HIS PAST, HIS FAMILY...
IT'S LIKE HE WANTS TO LEAVE IT ALL BEHIND.

WHY'RE YOU DEFENDING HIM?
C'MON, MOM.

THAT'S ...
...NOT TRUE.

I TOLD HIM THEY WERE MY FAVORITE.
THOSE FLOWERS ...
?

DAD REALLY SHOWED UP HERE?!

AND MY DOCTOR SAYS IT'S NOT A GOOD IDEA.
APPARENTLY, HE'S COME MANY TIMES.
THOUGH...WE HAVEN'T MET. I'M A BIT SCARED THOUGH...

ONLY ONCE.
BACK WHEN WE FIRST MET, I TOLD HIM.

NO. 187 - FLAMING ROAR! VS. NOMU: HIGH-END

WHOOOOSH

STAY ALERT! THIS GUY'S...
...JUST GETTING STARTED!
I'M NOT FLYING. MORE LIKE NOT FALLING.

I DIDN'T KNOW YOU COULD FLY, ENDEAVOR !!

PLUS... MAKING THIS ONE SOMETHING REAL SPECIAL, EVEN COMPARED TO THOSE OTHERS.

ARE YOU STRONG?
BWOOM
IT TALKS!!
WHICH MEANS...
FLASHFIRE FIST: HELL SPIDER!
I'LL TAKE YOU ALIVE AND MAKE YOU COUGH UP ALL YOU KNOW!
KZZZZZ
SHOOM
HWIP

HW
IP
SA
M

WHA-?!
KA-SLAM
KA-SLAM
...!!
THOOM

SZZZZ
FLASH
CHF
CHF
SSSS
SSSS
YANK
DOESN'T STAY BURNED FOR LONG...
SSS
SKF-SKF
GET IT TOGETHER, NUMBER ONE!
WHOA, THERE...
RRM
BBB
FLICK
FLICK

SW
GAAAAH!
BWOOM
IT'S FASTER AND STRONGER THAN ME?
EVEN REVERSE THRUST AIN'T ENOUGH...

THE WHOLE THING'S COMING DOWN!!
BB
MB
RR
RRMBBB
THIS'S LOOKING BAD!
THERE ARE STILL SO MANY PEOPLE IN THE BUILDING...
MBB
RR
B
RIGHT DOWN ONTO THE BUSY STREET!!
WAAA
QUIVER
AH!
FNA!

EVERY LITTLE VIBRATION THAT PEOPLE MAKE!
SCREAMS.
RUSTLING CLOTHES.
BREATHING.
...IN THE DAMAGED PART!!
ONLY THOSE PEOPLE WHO ARE...
I CAN'T MANAGE THE WHOLE BUILDING.
THERE AREN'T ENOUGH FEATHERS FOR THAT.
SENSE IT ALL, FEATHERS.
QUIVER
FIERCE WINGS!
HAWKS QUIRK:
TMP

THEY'RE SOLID ...
... YET GRACEFUL FEATHERS!
... EACH AND EVERY ONE OF THEM AT WILL!
AND HE CAN MANIP-ULATE ...
THUNK
THUNK
SHUNK
ALL 76 INDIVIDUALS HAVE BEEN REMOVED FROM THE DAMAGED PART OF THE BUILDING!
ENDEAVOR!!
SHUNK

KARTHOOM
CRUSH
TWIST
FUN-FUN...
NOT EVEN CLOSE!
IS THAT YOUR SHOW-STOPPER ?!

HERO

HAWKS (ZZ)

STREET CLOTHES

Birthday: 12/28
Height: 172 cm
Favorite Thing: Chicken (as food)

DEEP BEHIND THE SCENES

He was originally going to be a man with a bird head. Basically, the reappropriated design of Takahiro, from one of my older series. I'll be honest—I love bird people. You can blame *Mashin Hero Wataru* for that.

So how'd he get this human head? Well, during production of the movie, the anime staff came to me and asked, "Can we use Takahiro?" It was deeply moving to think that they had read my earlier series and wanted to show it some love. My life is basically peaking with this movie, so of course I agreed with enthusiasm. Not a big deal to change Hawks' design, after all.

After that, my staff had a lukewarm reaction to the idea of a birdman being number two, but I settled on this safe and sound (?) design for the guy.

BURN IT TO BITS!!
SHK SHK SHK
No. 188 - YOUR FATHER, THE NUMBER ONE HERO
WHOOSH
IN AN INSTANT ...
THAT'S GODLIKE!
HE'S CUTTING IT APART WITH FIRE!
SWISH
FWAH FWAH
ROLL ROLL ROLL
HAVEN'T ...
... YOU ...
...EVER COOKED ANYTHING, ENDEAVOR?

QUIT YAPPING AND TIGHTEN UP YOUR SLOPPY MOVES.
WHEN CHOPPING, YOU GOTTA MAKE THE PIECES UNIFORM.
Ouch!
THUD
THUD
YEAH, BUT WHEN I SEND OUT TOO MANY FEATHERS, MY FLYING TAKES A HIT.
WELL, EXCUSE ME!
BOOM
!
SWIP
BIRD...
SWIP
ENDEAVOR! HAWKS!! WE GOT YOUR BACKS!!
FWUMP
FWUMP
BWOOM
...INTER-INTERFERE.
BOOM
D-DON'T...
BOOM

- FLIES VIA **SHOULDER-MOUNTED JETS**
- **TRANSFORMING ARMS** AID IN FLIGHT BUT CAN ALSO STRETCH AND SPLIT APART
- STRETCHED-OUT ARMS ARE STRENGTHENED BY **MUSCULAR ENHANCEMENT**
- ENOUGH **POWER** TO SMASH STRAIGHT THROUGH REINFORCED CONCRETE
- PLUS **REGENERATION**

THAT MAKES FIVE!

AND THE SIXTH...

FISSION!

THEY'RE A DIFFERENT COLOR, THOUGH... SO MAYBE THEY'RE JUST STORED IN ITS BODY?

SO TO KEEP THE FIGHT WITH ME GOING, IT'S DIVERTING OUR BACKUP.
I'M REALLY STARTING TO OVERHEAT...
TAKING THIS THING AT FACE VALUE, IT'S OUT TO FIGHT SOMEONE STRONG. THAT'S PRETTY COMMON THINKING FOR VILLAINS!
...INTERFERED.
BOOM
TWIST
WHO'S THE BEST HERE?
FUN-FUN...
...THINKING!
THIS NOMU IS...
WORMP
WORMP
Grrah!
WAAAH! GET AWAY!!

SLASH!
FWAH
HAWKS!
WHOA!
YEP, IT'S ME.
NOW LET'S GET YOU GUYS SOMEWHERE NICE AND FAR AWAY.
BECAUSE IN ALL HONESTY, I CAN'T DO MUCH AGAINST BRUTE STRENGTH.
Gerahi
AND I AIN'T GUARANTEEING ANYTHING, ESPECIALLY WHEN IT'S MY OWN NECK ON THE LINE...

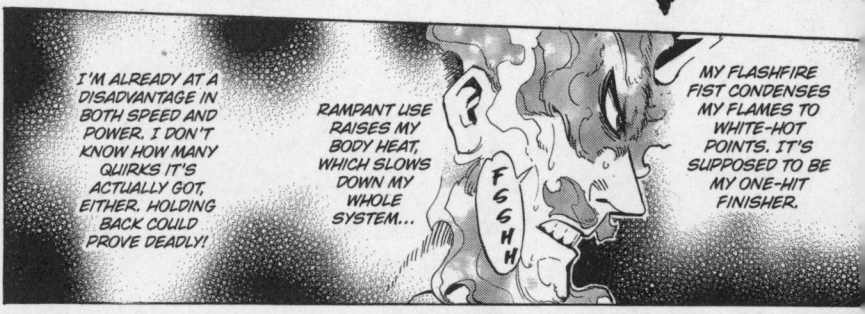

MY BODY JUST KEEPS OVERHEATING...

MY POWER!
MY-MY NEW...
...STR-STRENGTH.
SHP
SHP
LET-LET ME TRY IT ON Y-YOU!!
THERE!! DO YOU SEE HIM, FOLKS?! IT'S ENDEAVOR!!
SO BRIGHT, EVEN AT THIS DISTANCE!!
A PURGATORY YOU CAN'T ESCAPE OR REGENERATE FROM...
NOW, BURN AWAY TO NOTHING.
HE'S IGNITED, VIOLENTLY!!

PROMINENCE BURN!
I CAN'T LET YOU SEE ME BEING SO PATHETIC HERE!!
JUST WATCH ME!

SHZZ
ZZZ
FOOOOSH
WORMP

ENDEAVOR!
TOO BAD...
IT TORE IT OFF AND TOSSED IT?
THE HEAD...!
SHNK

AH!

I'M GOING TO TODOROKI.
KLICK

GUYS...
KEEP AN EYE ON ERI.
FWIP
LET'S TAKE A TRIP BACK TO YOUR ROOM, ERI.
?
OKAY.

ENDEAVOR ...!!

I'M HOPING TO BECOME A HERO YOU CAN BE PROUD OF...
NO STR-STRONGER HE-HEROES AROUND?
BOR-BORING.
YOUR FATHER, THE NUMBER ONE HERO.
OH, TODOROKI!
TODO-ROKI!
SOMEONE WHO DESERVES THAT TITLE...
GRR
VOLUME 20 - SCHOOL FESTIVAL START!! (END)

MY HERO ACADEMIA

reads from right to left, starting in the upper-right corner. Japanese is read from right to left, meaning that action, sound effects and word-balloon order are completely reversed from English order.

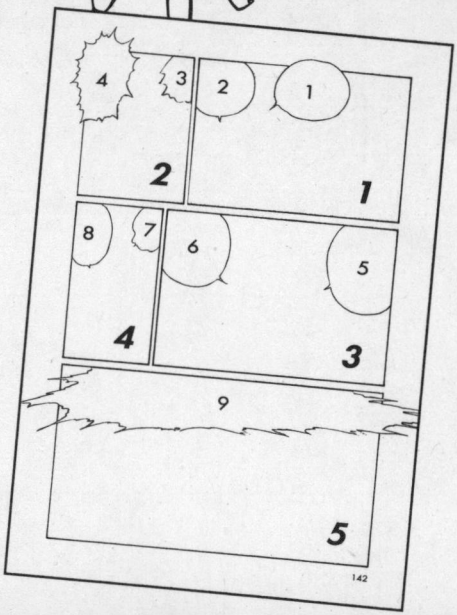